Lily of the Valley

Lily M. Morgan

This book is dedicated to my beautiful, kind and loving daughter Carol who sadly passed away on 13th March 2014.

Tears are never far away as we love her and miss her every day.

Carol

My daughter Carol was an angel on earth
No one could justifiably estimate her worth
She has worked hard all her life
An excellent caring daughter, mother and wife.

She was beautiful, intelligent, always helpful and kind
Attributes that cannot be bought to my mind
Of her numerous achievements I am so very proud
And wherever she was, she stood out in the crowd.

She was everything a daughter should be
And getting to look even more like me
I have countless memories to value and treasure
Of the happy times we had together.

Published by: Lily M. Morgan
Copyright © 2015 Lily M. Morgan
Design: Clive Davies Design
Printed by: Gwasg Dinefwr, Llandybie, Carmarthenshire

ISBN - 978-0-906821-82-4

Rugby

Have you ever watched a rugby match?
The full back jumps, the oval ball to catch
Men run and fight to score a try
And to this end they are prepared to die

Then of course there are the scrums
All you see are legs and bums
Oh to catch sight of a fleet footed winger
In full flight, a first class runner

Conceding penalties is the pits
Awarded points for successful kicks
A dropped goal however is much more fun
With such move great matches are won

The ball thrown straight towards the lineout
After the players coded shouts
Oh what bliss when it all goes right
And the ball is caught whilst in mid flight

Bloodied noses the game is rough
Broken bones the game is tough
But what the heck, it's only a game
What men will do for glory and fame

The Camera

All I've ever yearned for is a nice photo of me
But when I look at a camera, what is it that I see?
An alien one eyed monster glaring at me
At the ready to attack, to hurt and maim me

The result is so predictable, I simply look harassed
My sister Beryl gets annoyed and questions she does ask
What do you think you're doing? Is the obvious one
But when I see a camera I simply want to run

Beryl sits and poses and looks just like a star
Whilst I sit and appear to have been hit by a big car
What is wrong with me I often ask myself
As all my photos are kept hidden under the kitchen shelf

But I don't give up, I give it one more try
I look at the new photos, resigned I sit and cry
The camera will never love me, I now accept that this is true
I'll simply have to sit and gaze at beautiful photos of you

The Coal Mine

The coalmine was the hub of village life
Most of the men worked there, it was a life of strife
Coal was hewn but at what cost
Consider the total of all the lives lost

The miners who survived were old when young
Their breathing laboured from damaged lungs
Old men with flat caps on their haunches would sit
Discussing pigeons, chapels and working pits

Homeward bound, shedding attire
Washing in a zinc bath in front of the fire
Scrubbing themselves until it hurt
To rid their bodies of coal black dirt

Mountains of slag scarring the land
Music played by miners brass bands
All the children who died in Aberfan
Try to forget them if you can

These are my memories of my life in Wales
When the pits were closed, life changed in the vales
For the better I would say
On the day Margaret Thatcher had her way

The new generations will learn new skills
In cleaner jobs with fewer killed
So for us in Wales the future looks better
As this old tradition will no longer us fetter

Gossip

Mari number four is pregnant again
Doesn't she ever remember the pain?
Who the father is, I don't think she knows
It could be one of three or four beaus
Am I a gossip? No, I am not!

Mrs. Jones number eight
Went to the Doctor but she'd left it too late
An examination showed that her appendix had burst
They took her to hospital, it could have been worse
Am I a gossip? No, I am not!

Have you heard about her at number three?
She went to Swansea on a shoplifting spree
They found the goods inside her bag
The Police prosecuted and kept the swag
Am I a gossip? No, I am not!

Mrs. Evans keeps all those cats
Why does she bother, she's still got the rats
She's got 'Beware of the Dog' on her front gate
Yet all that dog does is eat and mate
Am I a gossip? No, I am not!

Mrs. Rees is in debt to the shop
She'd bought some fags and crisps and pop
But could she pay for them? No, she could not
She's a bad one, that one, her and her lot
Am I a gossip? No, I am not!

Poor Dora is disconcerted
She's just had a ring inserted
It's purpose is to hold everything up
Just like a bra with a double D cup
Am I a gossip? No, I am not!

Freddie next door is the village ram
He had it off with my cousin Pam
His father Ted was worse, much worse
He had to be treated by the Nurse
Am I a gossip? No, I am not!

The Custom and Excise also called at Number three
They were caught smuggling Duty Free
Fags and Booze filled every room
The future for them is all doom and gloom
We could really do without their kind
They lower the tone of the street to my mind
Am I a gossip? No, I am not!

Sister

I must look after my younger sister
Even though she's a little trickster
For she is weak and I am strong
And in Mama's eyes, she can do no wrong

She is spoilt every single day
Mama lets her have her way
For she is weak and I am strong
She is always right and I am always wrong

It's no fun being the older sister
It means I'm not allowed to hit her
For she is weak and I am strong
And I must never do her wrong

To have her own way, she goes to cry
She only has to ask and Mama will buy
For she is weak and I am strong
I just think it's very wrong

My youngest sister is a spoilt little brat
All except Mama can see that
For she is weak and I am strong
And in Mama's eyes she can do no wrong

Parting

God called my name, do not weep for me
From pain and suffering he set me free
He took my hand, he showed me the way
To his heavenly abode, he bade me stay

I go to a better place, a happier life
Everyone joyful, no hunger, no strife
Do not weep for me, I was ready to leave
Remember the good times, do not grieve

Grieving is the price we pay
For loved ones, on the parting of the ways
All I ask is that you occasionally think of me
And smile at all the memories

Speed

Live life in the fast lane, it's the only way
Daily I ride my motorcycle, along the Welsh highway
Wearing my leathers, crash helmet on my head
Swerving and veering, as the traffic lights not red

I am a speed addict, racing in my veins
Those thirty miles an hour drivers, I view with great distain
They don't know the feeling of blood coursing through their veins
Heart thumping in their chests, exhilaration causing pain
Live life in the fast lane, it's the only way

A motorcyclist I may be but I know the danger
I know that my mam worries as I am her beloved teenager
'Speed Kills' she often tells me, I smile and say 'I know'
I then put on my gear and astride my bike I go
Live life in the fast lane, it's the only way

Another day, the wather's fine
I feel the itch, it's time to ride
My Kawasaki, my pride and joy, what bliss!
Life doesn't get much better than this
I increase my speed, turn a corner...
SPEED KILLS

A Tree

Why don't you stand and look at a tree
Standing in a field so majestically
Leafily clad, resplendent in green
Some hiding nests, not easily seen

Branches spread out, forming a bower
A haven to shelter during a shower
Or a shaded area to escape the sun
To such a place the animals run

During the autumn the leaves change colour
To brown, orange, rust when the weather is duller
Soon branches are bare, as leaves go astray
Nests are deserted, the birds flown away

Wearing a winter coat of snow
Heavily laden, the branches bow
A tree however, is a beautiful sight
Even when green is replaced by white

Brains

I am not beautiful and this I regret
When I look in the mirror I get upset
However, I've got a first class degree
Why is it then, that men ignore me?

Men prefer a blonde bimbo without a brain
Someone superficial and ever so vain
What is wrong with men that they cannot see?
Beauty fades, she'll end up like me

Brainpower however, forever lasts
Bounteous assets I have amassed
I have aged well, as is always the case
Men should look ahead when young girls they chase

Bless This House

Bless this house oh Lord I pray
As my friends are coming to stay
The four of them, they are a bind
I must have been not of sound mind

First there is Nora, she is a bitch
Even though she's filthy rich
She is fussy about the food she eats
Doesn't like chips, won't eat meat

Then there is Bessy, she is a snob
She will look down on all I have got
I'll really have to treat her the best
Give her more than all the rest

Marjorie is the jealous one
She will be moody and not much fun
I can't help it that I am her better
I shouldn't have sent her the damn letter

Last but not least is Rosie the thief
I'll have to put everything out of reach
She is also untidy and not very clean
Doesn't like to wash or preen

Bless this house oh Lord I pray
They are my friends, they are welcomed to stay
I hope that I will cope each day
I won't invite them in a hurry again

Wales

I would die for Wales, the land of my birth
Only the Welsh value its worth
The mountains and vales, the culture too
Occupied and embraced by the very few

The beaches, the towns, the buildings, the streets
The friendliness exuded as tourists we greet
Welsh artists famous around the world
Singers, Actors spreading the word

Great progress has been made, we have become well known
Welsh communities abroad have thrived and grown
The Welsh émigrés are Welsh through and through
Their patriotism remaining strong and true

Welsh we are born and Welsh we will stay
We have survived tough times along the way
As Dafydd Iwan sings 'We are still here'
And intend remaining so in this land we hold dear

The Flu

It is dreadful to feel so ill
Do I need to make a will?
I have caught that flu from Fiji
I fear that it's trying to kill me

I don't feel well, my body aches
Some medicine and pills I'll have to take
My doctor said to stay in bed
As my temperature is high and my cheeks are red

Coughing all day, coughing all night
My sides are aching, my chest is tight
Antibiotics, they need time to work
As in my body viruses lurk

I am feeling weak but I have started to eat
Beginning to stand on my own two feet
Hope springs eternal, I am feeling better
I must send my Doctor a 'Thank You' letter

A Spot

A spot is a very nasty thing
Squeeze it and you'll feel it sting
Or you can leave it 'til it bursts
I don't quite know which is the worse

If you have one on your face
To the chemist you must race
Otherwise you'll have a scar
You mustn't let it get that far

If your rear end is numb
You've probably got one on your bum
Put a poultice on it soon
Else it will prevent you moon

If you are spotty don't despair
We all sympathise, as we've been there
As one day your spots will disappear
Leaving your skin smooth and clear

Bliss

My money I have spent
A small house I must rent
The DHSS will pay
No taxes I will pay
Oh what bliss
To have achieved this
All on my very own
Because wild oats I've sown

My money, it just went
My savings, I just spent
I lived for each day
In luxury, my way
Now the money's gone
Was what I did so wrong?
The DHSS will pay
And no taxes I will pay

Secret

A secret you must keep
To no one, you repeat
T'was for your ears alone
You were the one she chose

To tell would break her heart
From your life she would depart
Her secret you will keep
As your friendship doth run deep

Fear

I'm scared, I'm scared, I'm really scared
There is a wild animal somewhere out there
Roaming the countryside here in Wales
Killing animals in the dales

What would I do if I met it one night?
Would I stand rigid or would I take flight
I think I'd lie down and pretend to be dead
Otherwise it'll escape extremely well fed

Toy Boy

I have got a toy boy, he's a lot younger than me
Why he chose me is a mystery
He is young and handsome and very active
Whilst I need a facelift to make me attractive

Alas he is poor, I'm the one with the money
The way we met, well it was uncanny
He asked if he could mow my lawn
And before it was finished true love was born

Bare chested in shorts I watched him pose
I went weak at the knees as my blood pressure rose
My hormones unbalanced ran amok
And my poor old body went into shock

He loves me to bits, he tells me this every day
And I have adapted to younger ways
It is a pity I've now got this bad back
And yesterday I had an asthmatic attack
Is all the excitement too much for me?
No, of course not, I'll cope, my doctor I'll see

My friends don't like him and that makes me sad
I know they are jealous when they say that he's bad
They tried to stop me changing my will
Saying that he'd gone in for the kill
They say it's a scandal, that gossip is rife
They don't understand, he has changed my life

I bought him a car, I bought him a bike
Because I know they are things that he likes
I have got a toy boy twenty years younger than me
Don't you women all wish that you were me!

Busybody

They say that I'm a busybody, but I know that isn't true
I just like to know what's going on with people like you
I know I take an interest, I think it's a good thing
Cos if I saw a robbery, the policeman I would ring

I wonder if her next door has got a fancy man
I know that Peter the Baker visits as often as he can
And then of course there is that boy she calls her big mistake
He's a right old so and so, always on the take

Opposite me live that rowdy lot, I hear them scream and shout
What else can they do with fourteen children about
They claim all the benefits going, he doesn't need to work
They've got a slimline telly and in the drive a Merc

I've reached a milestone in my life, I've got to move from here
Find a better class of people where I'll try not to interfere
I'd give them each a jar of my homemade strawberry jam
Give them a chance to get to know the nice person that I am
They will invite me in of course, then I can have a look
To see what kind of place they've got and discover if they can cook

I live alone and it is sad that it's come to this
Me peering behind the curtains in case there's something that I'll miss
They say that I'm a busybody but that just isn't true
I know it, my friends know it, and now so do you

My Operation

I occupied a bed
In Prince Phillip Hospital, it must be said
I'd been having problems with my rear end
Piles were blocking my colonic S bend

Down to the theatre to have my op
Into a container the offending items did drop
When I came to, there was a drip by my bed
Into my vein the saline was fed

Turned on your side, bottom up
It was embarrassing I'd had more than enough
Doctors peering at my posterior
Well, it all made me feel a little peculiar

My hospital stay, it was really a pleasure
All my time was spend in leisure
Smiling at visitors, reading a book
A little courage was all it took

Now at home, I can't sit, it hurts to go to the loo
I keep taking paracetamols, wouldn't you?
If any of you suffer from this complaint
An operation, be warned, pleasant it ain't

Birth

I have just been born and what do I see
A strange face, two weary eyes looking at me
All of a sudden I'm held upside down
By my ankles, frightened I frown
Someone slaps me, I don't know why
Shocked and angry I start to cry
I don't like this place, I feel so cold
Poor little me, I'm only a few minutes old

It has all been traumatic for someone my size
A once in a lifetime experience, I'm just glad I survived
Suddenly things are better, I've been given a wash
Wrapped in a blanket I feel quite posh
Someone weeps and holds me real close
I feel warm and secure in silent repose
Contented I snuggle and fall asleep
The worst is over, I've been born, tomorrow will keep

One or Two

You need two to be a twin
Yet only one person to win
You need two to fall in love
Only one God in heaven above
You need two to speak on the phone
One person to stand alone
You need two to kiss
One girl can be a Miss
You need two to wed
One person to sleep in a single bed
What does it matter if it's one or two
Buy one get one free, then you'll have two

Recognition

Beauty is in the eye of the beholder, so it is said
It could be a girl with red hair on her head
Or possibly a flower in full bloom
Or a tapestry hanging on the wall in a room

Beauty however, is recognised by all
See it, know it, and in love you fall
Be it a painting, a car or a Ming
Large sums of money are paid for such things

Inner beauty surpasses all, without thought
It is priceless and it cannot be bought
It is flawless and it lasts forever
Can you acquire it? The answer unfortunately is never

Storms

The skies darken, it doesn't look good
I wear a mac with a matching hood
Then it starts pouring, torrential rain
With gale force winds, so fierce they pain
I'm windswept and soaked, so home I must go
To sit in front of the fire, with embers aglow
Only fools venture out prior to a storm
The wise ones stay in, dry, cosy and warm

What about sandstorms in the desert
Sand darkening the sky, no daylight present
Sand in your eyes, your hair, your nose
In such circumstance, lie in covered repose
Once the storm is over, get out of there, fast
As another sandstorm could be your last

What about those storms in teacups
Petty squabbles between grownups
They are nothing at all to do with the weather
To reach a compromise they should endeavour
We must protect ourselves from these storms
Stay at home, safe in our own private dorms

Pleasure

Little things give pleasure, memories to treasure
A kiss on the hand, now isn't that grand?
A single red rose from someone you know
A small box filled with your favourite sweets
A shared bottle of wine, now that's quite a treat
A kiss on the cheek from someone you meet
A kiss on the lips from someone you've missed
Yet sometimes all it takes is a smile
To give a little pleasure

Beauty

Beauty is all around us, we only have to look
At a new born baby or a babbling brook
A rainbow in the sky with its colourful hue
Or a spider's web glistening with dew

A garden full of flowers, their fragrance to imbibe
Lambs prancing in the fields, no words can them describe
Blue skies and white clouds a painting do portray
A waterfall cascading sending water on its way

These are gifts of nature, made to brighten up our day
Alas we are all too busy, these wondrous things to assay
Beauty is all around us, we only have to look
In Spring, Summer, Autumn, Winter, we only have to look

My Garden

My garden is a joy to me
It's where I watch things grow
And during March and April, the seeds I plant and sow
Subsequently, flowers appear, a colourful display
To inspire me and cheer me on damp and dismal days

There is a seat up in my garden, where I rest and ponder
Talking to departed ones, my mind begins to wander
Remembering the good times and the bad times too
Wondering what it was all about and the love I had for you

I sit and watch the butterflies, floating in the air
And the little robins as they boldly stand and stare
A family of foxes visit now and then
Three cubs playing on the lawn, having left their den
The parents keep a watchful eye, in case things get too rough
And silently they all depart, when they have had enough

My garden is a joy to me, it's hard work to keep it neat
The lawns, the hedges, buildings, the task is no mean feat
But it is my haven, my shelter from life's storm
Where strains and stresses are released and life returns to norm.

Speed Dating

To go speed dating you need to be a good sport
So I went along to the venue where they weekly hold court
I sat at a table, spoke to a man for ten seconds
In a flash he was gone and another man beckoned

I made a note of his name, he didn't me impress
I didn't like his hair or his mode of dress
He wore an orange shirt for goodness sake
Had a ponytail and a beard that covered most of his face

Along came a young man called Jeremy
He didn't say a word, just stared at me
I did all the talking and that just isn't my way
One thing's for sure he didn't make my day

The next one was a professor, now he was really my kind
It was the meeting of two superior minds
We discussed the environment, also Brown and Blair
Disagreed on the economy, so I got up and left him there
The problem was he wouldn't see my point of view
Men!! What's new?

This one looks promising I said to myself
He was confident, appeared to have wealth
He was tall and handsome although a little dim
I immediately thought I wouldn't mind sleeping with him
But when he told me that he suffered from gout
That was it, I'd had enough I got up and walked out

Speed dating evidently is not my thing
I was looking for more than a fling
I shouldn't have worn that mini skirt, it was a little tight
And going by the men's reactions, I must have looked a sight
Common sense prevails however; I'll have to keep on looking around
Surely, somewhere, there's a good man to be found

Roses

A cultivated flower with a thorny stem
A red one chosen as the English emblem
A beauty said to be an English Rose
Is blonde and blue eyed as described in prose

A single red rose given to a loved one
Telling her your heart she has won
Roses also come in yellow, pink or white
In full bloom a wonderful sight

A beautiful flower, watch the thorny stem
You have to be careful how you pick them
You will bleed if you prick your finger
The pain will go away but the fragrance will linger

Lazy

I open one eye, look at the clock
I am lying in bed, it is twelve o'clock
Shall I stay in bed or shall I get up?
I switch on the teasmaid, I'll have a cup

I think I will laze for another hour
Then I'll have a refreshing shower
It is afternoon, I sit and watch TV
I ring for a takeaway, delivered to me

It is early evening, I am having a rest
I want to look my very best
As my lover is planning to visit
His stay is always very illicit

I haven't cleaned the house, but he won't mind
He understands that I am very refined
So what does it matter if the house is a mess
He knows I hate housework and this I confess

My mother will call tomorrow and do all the work
She will hoover and dust, she thinks I'm a jerk
She will wash and iron, all for free
Who is the wisest? Her or me?

Chocolate

It was my birthday yesterday
My friend gave me a box of chocolates, it is her way
Shall I open it? I'll eat only the one
I am on a diet which isn't much fun

Which one shall I have? The hazelnut for sure
Oh that was nice, I'll have a liqueur
The orange, the coconut, the Turkish delight
I think I'd better put the box out of sight

My body is strong but the spirit is weak
There is no way this box will last me all week
How many are left? Oh just the two
I might as well eat the lot, a treat from Sue

Pain

A pain is an ache that you try to ignore
Ignore it at your peril, of this I am sure
A pain is a symptom that something is wrong
You must see the Doctor, you've got to be strong
If it is serious, the sooner the better
Then the pain and the worry will no longer you fetter

For Old Time's Sake

It has been a while so I'm sending you this letter
To arrange a meeting, what could be better?
A day at the most, it will only take
A little get together for old time's sake

You were my lover, you were my best friend
And on you I could always depend
We could go back to that restaurant by the lake
A little get together for old time's sake

Please don't say 'No', it would break my heart
We have been too long apart
Just one meeting, that is all it will take
A little get together for old time's sake

A Smile

White gleaming teeth, a beautiful smile
Given to someone you haven't seen for a while
This smile however, it don't come cheap
As to the Dentist, cheque book in hand, you reluctantly creep

A little filling here, a large one there
Mouth agape at the drill you stare
Everything numb so that you don't feel the pain
In due course, a beautiful smile you will gain

The person who never smiles is an unhappy soul
Whose passions and feelings have turned icy cold
What is the answer you may well ask
To rekindle happiness is a difficult task

It is not the end of the world however
Friendship and encouragement should be your endeavour
The day will come when the sun will shine
and we will once again see that beautiful smile

World War II

I was a child when war broke out
But I still remember the rallying shout
'Your country needs you' were the words that were said
All the young men to the slaughter were led
Thousands died in foreign lands
The British were proud, we had made a stand
We had stopped Hitler's armies in their tracks
Montgomery had marshalled our army's tanks

Churchill's V sign and cigar
Inspired the Country, the best leader by far
I also recall the London blitz
Coventry and Swansea were badly hit
German planes droning overhead
Running to air raid shelters, leaving warm beds
We carried gas masks in little square boxes
A safeguard against germ warfare and toxins

Air raid sirens, ration books
A strong back bone was all it took
Land Army girls working the land
Doctors and Nurses meeting demands
Security in Britain was very tight
Blackouts on windows to hide the light
Policemen and Firemen did their bit too
To ensure the safety of me and you

When it was over, what a relief
It cost us dear, it was beyond belief
All the young men who never came back
Who valiantly died whilst under attack
Their sacrifices however, were not in vain
Our freedom was won, we kept our Domain
It does make one wonder what is wrong with man?
War is beyond my comprehension, man killing man

A Letter

I've got to write a letter and send it off today
To my friend in Australia, a land that's far away
I really must tell her about my fall
And how my leg got broke
And that our dear friend Marie Rose has had a minor stroke
She needs to know that her old boyfriend John has suddenly passed away
From Pleurisy and Pneumonia, so the papers say

I'll say that all her friends have had a get together
A reunion dinner in the Glamorgan Arms
And things just couldn't get better
We are all going to Majorca, without her, it is true
But we all think of her often and love and miss her too

Our syndicate has won the lottery, a hundred thousand ponds
We intend to go out shopping, buying jewellery and gowns
I know that she will be pleased for us, we all wish that she were here
But I'm certain that this letter of mine will leave her in good cheer

Woman

A woman is a complex being
Guided by maternal feeling
This is something all males lack
Finding femininity difficult to hack

These feelings are advantageous to the men
As initially women want to mother them
Love them, care for them, cater to their needs
Subsequently, have their children, to nurture and to feed

A woman is a complex being, in some respects unique
She can make a big strong man, buckle at the knees
With the right man at her side she can conquer all
Keep the ship afloat whilst letting him stand tall

The Telly

I relax in my chair to watch the telly
Eating sweets, hugging my belly
David Jason is on as Inspector Jack Frost
Catching criminals much to their cost

Emmerdale's Cain
Inflicting pain
Coronation Street's Fred
He ended up dead
Eastenders Dot and Jim
And Nigel Harman, I won't forget him

S4C is the channel for me
Pobl Y Cwm I never fail to see
Marian and Denzil in that shop
Dai Sgaffaldi caught on the hop
Hywel the handsome womaniser
And Kath the reliable home provider

I always watch Scrum V on BBC2
The Scarlets scoring a try or two
After the ITV News, Mark Austin always me thanks
For watching knife culture in action and soldiers in tanks

The telly holds pride of place in my home
As these days I am unable to roam
To me and my kind it is a godsend
As for News and Entertainment, on it we depend

My Piano

I sit at my piano, look at the keys
Which key shall I play in, I'll try the 'C'
It is the easiest, no black notes to play
I choose a song and play it my way

It gives me great pleasure, my piano
I wish I could play a piano concerto
However, my talent is very limited
I play for my friends, it is appreciated

I don't need music, it is all in my head
Self taught, on the keys my fingers are led
The keys of D, E, F and G, I also know
But to accomplished pianists my head I bow

Piano lessons I wish I'd had
I just grew up when times were hard
God in his goodness gave me the talent to play
My piano, I care for and use everyday

Debt

I owe money here, I owe money there

I owe so much, I no longer care
The problem was all the things that I bought
Using my cards, without a thought
Where it will end, I just don't know
To the Citizens Advice Bureau I'll have to go

OH I'm so happy, my debts I have cleared
It wasn't half as hard as I feared
I paid off a little sum each week
Stopped buying things I didn't need
My friends helped out, kept me away from the shops
I am just so pleased I've come out on top

Stubborn

I've always been stubborn, my mother said
I refuse to conform, I'm not easily led
In my opinion it is a good thing
As to my true self I steadfastly cling

My mother's tried knocking me into shape
As my sisters I refused to ape
I am me, I speak my mind
I resist her chastisement, I am one of a kind

It would be boring if we were all the same
I only have myself to blame
This trait, I have inherited from someone
My headstrong mother for sure, she's the one

I am so stubborn, I refuse to give in
Sometimes I wonder if it is a good thing
The hassle, the beatings I have endured
I could well do without, of that I am sure

Ingrained, however, it is here to stay
I am opinionated, it is my way
It does, however, stand me in good stead
As against all opposition, I am not easily led

The Lottery

Six numbers I have chosen, multiplied by four
Hoping that a fortune will come knocking on my door
In my head I've already spent the money, given some away
Oh I hope and pray that a win will come my way

I've already won ten pounds, several times it's true
These trivial little sums, however, simply will not do
I really want a big, big, win, so I can spend at leisure
On houses, cars and holidays, it would give me so much pleasure

I am also in a syndicate, I pay one pound a week
We are all united, a gigantic win we seek
Twenty pounds it costs for twenty lines each week
Very costly, but if you ain't in it, you can't win it

Every week I'm disappointed, end up feeling blue
Yet every Monday I shop and buy three tickets new
I am hooked on the lottery, afraid to let it go
As it could be my turn next to win a lot of dough

Utopia

Wouldn't it be nice if we lived in a world without cruelty or sorrow
Without poverty, sickness, cancer or aids, and no worries about tomorrow
Where children could play and go out alone, without fear of abuse or abduction
Where nations would unite for the good of mankind
and a peaceful existence would function
Selfishness and greed become a thing of the past and starvation resolved forever
Will this utopia ever emerge? In the present climate... Never!

Crying

If someone is kind to me, I start to cry
Kindness I cannot accept, I don't know why
If someone shouts at me, I react, I attack
A natural defence, though physical strength I lack
Why should that be?

Crocodile tears of course, women employ
Is this crying genuine or a female ploy?
A clever use of tears to let them have their way
Men must learn to know the difference, or the price they'll pay
Why should that be?

There are tears of happiness when good news comes your way
There are tears of sorrow when your lover starts to stray
Persistent crying is a sign of severe black depression
Medical help and friends, the pressure they can lessen
Crying is an expression of feeling
Why should that be?

A River

A little trickle of water on a mountain high
Downwards flowing as rain falls from the sky
Gaining momentum, widening on its way
It soon becomes a river where fresh water fish hold sway

There are famous rivers, in Egypt there's the Nile
The longest river in Africa, it flows for miles and miles
In London they have the Thames, In Germany the Rhine
And in France of course they have the river Seine

A river is one of nature's wonders
Over cliffs the waterfall's thunder
A more beautiful sight I have yet to behold
As that of a river, uncontrolled

Kim

I lost a very good friend today
I shed some tears when they took her away
She had been a lifelong friend to me
She was entitled to die with dignity

She pushed her way into my heart
She licked my face, it was a good start
A very good house dog she became
She was my pet, Kim was her name

She was special, even though of mixed breed
She was everything one could possibly need
Companion, protector, all in one
She took me for walks, we also had fun

She was feeble and old when the vet put her to sleep
She is buried in my garden, there I her keep
Her loyalty and devotion I had to repay
I'll always remember the dog who came my way

The Farm

Have you seen the animals on the farm?
They won't do you any harm
There are cows and pigs and cats
Horses, dogs and also rats
There are chickens and some goats
Rabbits, hamsters and wild stoats
Do pay a visit to a farm
You won't come to any harm

Too Late

I only needed one minute of your time to tell you that I loved you
I only needed one minute of your time to tell you that I cared
The problem is you're gone, I left it all too late
All I have left is disillusionment and hate

It started off so promising on the day we met
We were young and optimistic, you played hard to get
But fall in love we did and made our vows for life
We were so happy when you became my loving wife

The daily grind just got too much, you found it hard to bear
I was always absent, too busy to be there
Then to my horror I came home to find you gone
Bereft and all alone, I found the sun no longer shone

I only needed one minute of your time to convince you that I loved you
I only needed one minute of your time to convince you that I cared
But love needs to be fuelled to endure and survive
All I have are memories as all alone I strive

Cinema

To the cinema I used to go
Every Saturday with my friend Flo
A bag of sweets bought in the foyer
I became a cinematic voyeur

On the waterfront with Marlon Brando
Omar Shariff as Doctor Zhivago
Watching Paul Newman or John Wayne
Red Indians inflicting torturous pain

Ava Gardner with Clark Gable
Lana Turner wearing sable
Susan Hayword and Tyrone Power
Janet Leigh killed in that shower

The Great Escape with Steve McQueen
The motorbike chase the best I've seen
Burton and Taylor that romantic pair
Ginger Rogers, Fred Astaire

Nelson Eddy the Canadian Mounty
Clint Eastwood chasing crooks for bounty
Robert Taylor in Quo Vadis
Sean Connery and Richard Harris

They don't make films like that anymore
Although Gladiator with Crowe is quite a show
I could go on forever and ever
Will I ever forget them? The answer is never!

A Friend

You are very lucky if you have a friend
Someone always there for you, one on whom you can depend
Your worries she will share, your secrets she will keep
And when you are despondent on her shoulder you will weep

Even when you're happy she will share your joy
She will sing your praises, with her you won't be coy
She will be honest, her judgement will be sound
An achiever you'll become as her encouragement abounds

If you have a friend, cherish her and care
Enjoy her company as many interests you do share
A genuine true friend is worth her weight in gold
When God made her, he threw away the mold

A Blazer

A blazer is so useful, you can wear it with a skirt
A man can also wear one over a trousers and clean shirt
It is like a uniform as it looks so smart
With a decorated pocket, right over the wearers heart

It can be any colour, navy, black, red or blue
You just go ahead and choose the one for you
Blazers are worn by the working class, also the elite
I daresay you know of someone wearing one in your street

As a fashion statement, the blazer reigns supreme
Worn at the Olympics and also by football teams
The David Beckham's of this world, also royalty
Give the useful blazer their undying loyalty

A Tail

A tail is a very funny thing stuck at the rear end
Most animals have one, it is the one thing they can't bend
Monkeys often use them to swing from tree to tree
And dogs will wag their tails, if they like the look of me
A horse will swish his tail to drive away flies
The squirrel has the bushiest, one he's unable to disguise
A tail is a very funny thing, stuck right there on the end
But the animals right to have one, I'll defend to the bitter end

Time

There is a time for everything
A time to cry, a time to sing
A time to rest, a time to have fun
A time to walk, time to run

There is a time to sleep, a time to get up
Call it a day when you've had enough
A time to quarrel, a time to make up
A time to talk, a time to shut up

There is a time to win, never to lose
And in affairs of the heart, time to choose
A time to stay, a time to leave
And on the parting of the ways, time to grieve

There is a time to work, a time to rest
A time to accept, a time to protest
A time for truth, a time to lie
A time to live, a time to die

Romanies

Romanies are born to roam
Caravans their mobile homes
Continually moving from place to place
No peace for this nomadic race

They have been around for umpteen years
Their mere presence sparking fears
Their lifestyle is a blot on the landscape
The disruption, the mess, one cannot escape

But who are we to judge their mode
As they continue life's way, travelling roads
Should they be persecuted because they differ
Washing clothes and bathing, in nature's rivers

We are all God's people and life is short
We should endeavour the problems to sort
Co-exist in harmony, aim for peace
Tolerance on both sides would appease

Gold Age Pensioner

I am a gold age pensioner, that really surprised me
It was on today's news, the BBC
It is a term I've never heard before
What it means I'm really not sure

I've got a small car, I've got my health
But where, I ask, is all that wealth?
I own my house, I've loads of friends
My lifestyle is good and that I'll defend
But a gold age pensioner, surely that cannot be
But they are referring to you and me

I've worked all my life and saved really hard
Consequently, from free handouts I am now debarred
With interest rates low, my savings have dwindled
I'm really cheesed off, I feel I've been swindled
But all of a sudden, I feel a lot better
As I've just been told I am a real go-getter

Do you know what it's like?

Do you know what it's like
To go for a ride on a motorbike
Speeding on the highway, the wind in your hair
Wearing shades to avoid the sun's glare
Holding on tight to the one that you trust
This exhilarating experience is a must
Well I know what it's like

Do you know what it's like
To go on a cruise down the River Nile
Gazing at the pyramids in the scorching sun
The ugly smelly Camels not much fun
Visiting the museum in the capital Cairo
The Tutankhamen exhibits inciting sorrow
Well I know what it's like

Do you know what it's like
To stand on a stage holding a mike
Reciting some poems, singing some songs
Praying in your heart that things won't go wrong
Oh what bliss on hearing the applause
For a performance with no obvious flawes
Well I know what it's like

Do you know what it's like
To be spoilt rotten by the man in your life
Receive breakfast in bed every day
Bouquets of flowers coming your way
Being given boxes of chocolates, Cadbury's Milk Tray
Agreeing with everything that you say
Well no!! I don't know what it's like

Daughter in Law

She is the daughter in law from hell
What made my son choose her, I cannot tell
She can't cook, doesn't clean, can't make decent food
But worse than that, to me she is rude

I am her better before I get out of bed in the morning
She is so devious, so clever, I tried to warn him
But love is blind, he ignored my advice
And now of course, he is paying the price

I worry about him, I visit every day
Trying to get her to do things my way
I've got to keep an eye on my little boy
As this marriage has brought him no joy

I lose sleep as she spends all his money
Mostly on fags and I don't think it's funny
I know she is jealous that I am a woman of means
I refuse to eat her toast and baked beans

She told me I was the mother in law from hell
Can you believe it? It made me unwell
He is blind to her faults, I'll just have to persevere
To right all her wrongs, as he will never leave her

She is the daughter in law from hell that one!

Loneliness

I am alone, I stare at the walls
I look at the phone, no one calls
I gaze out of the window, there is no one there
I just exist in this awful nightmare

I must do something, I am going out of my mind
Take up a hobby, my thoughts to unwind
Listen to music, or a book I must read
The symptoms of depression I'll have to heed

This loneliness is hard to take
Some friends I'll have to cultivate
The alternative is to have a pet
A loyal friendly dog I will have to get

Walking the dog, I met this man
He is very nice, although no Don Juan
His dog likes my dog, I can tell
So the four of us get on really well

If you are lonely and feeling sad
Take a leaf out of my book, there's a life to be had
You alone can turn your world around
As out there, friends can be found

Bluebells

A carpet of blue
A colourful hue
Surrounding the trees
Swaying in the breeze, bluebells supreme

Absence

Where are you? You are not here
I am uneasy, your absence I fear
You may have met someone new
Forgotten how much I love you

Where are you my love, you are not here
I wish, oh how I wish that you were here
Then I could tell you how much I care
That a love like ours is very rare

No Fixed Abode

I have no kith or kin
I sleep amongst bins
My life is spent on the road
I am of - no fixed abode

Please don't think I am bad
As face begrimed I look dejected and sad
It wasn't always like this, I'll have you know
I am down and out, my head bowed low

I have lost touch with family and friends
On kindred spirits and handouts I now depend
I spend all my days on the road
As I am of – no fixed abode

An Idea

I've just had an idea
What it is isn't clear
I know it's there, in my head
It just hasn't come to me yet
So I'll just have to wait
As a brainwave it ain't

A Little White Lie

She looked bedraggled, I told her she looked good
To make her feel better, as one should
The effect was dramatic, she stopped being shy
All because I told – a little white lie

She was a little dim, I told her she was bright
She took the test and did alright
She smiled and gave a satisfied sigh
All because I told – a little white lie

She came home late
A good hiding was her fate
I lied, said she was early, she had no cause to cry
All because I told – a little white lie

Dreaming

In a beautiful house, I would like to live
Have plenty of money, so parties I'd give
Have Arabian horses in my well kept stables
Wearing clothes with designer labels

I can daydream I suppose
Stops me feeling sad and morose
It helps me cope with the daily grind
Feeling that life is extremely unkind

In a beautiful house, I would like to live

The Circus

The circus is in town
I've just seen the boisterous clowns
Large bulbous noses, painted faces
Wearing large buckled shoes without any laces

The trapeze artists swaying on swings
Aloft in the air, they fly without wings
With hearts in our mouths, we watch them let go
How they don't fall, we really don't know

The lion's roar as they prowl in their cage
At a crack of the whip they show their rage
They are magnificent animals who should be free
Yet they are entertaining, you and me

Scantily dressed beauties riding on horseback
As horses gallop around the ring's track
Jugglers throwing balls in the air
Hatchets sometimes thrown, by those who dare

The circus is in town, it will stay a week
I've just seen them, parading down our street
The artists, the animals, a wonderful sight
Under the big top, we'll pay to watch them tonight

Need

You need money to buy
You need tears to cry
You need eyes to see
You need a cup to have tea

You need ears to hear
You need a scare to know fear
You need a tongue to speak
You'll need loss of strength to feel weak

You need teeth to chew
You need people to queue
You need legs to stand
You need gloves to warm hands

You need an ache to feel pain
You need royalty to reign
You need an infection to be diseased
You need to die to be deceased

An Actress

An actress I would like to be
Someone else, other than me
A beautiful maiden rescued by a knight
A warrior queen, flexing her might
Wearing a bikini meeting James Bond
Swimming with Costner in a lake or pond
As Cleopatra sailing down the Nile
At Richard Burton I would smile
An actress I would like to be
Someone else, other than me

Night Sky

I like to look at the sky at night
To see all those stars shining bright
If I'm lucky, a falling star I'll see
Or a new moon to dazzle me
Red sky at night is the shepherd's delight
To us as well it is a glorious sight

Books

I am an avid reader to the library I go
Every month I read three books, sometimes four
Murder mysteries and spies are my favourite ones
Tom Sharpe's "Blot on the Landscape" was hilarious fun

John Grisham was a lawyer and this his book reflects
"The Firm" and "The Client" show him at his very best
Catherine Cookson's heroines always end up rich
She introduced the mallen streak and "The Whip"

James Patterson however is the best
Head and Shoulders above the rest
"Roses are Red", "Violets are Blue"
Two excellent books I would recommend to you

J K Rowling's Harry Potter, Jeffrey's Archer's Kane and Abel
Jilly Cooper "Riders" about horses, riders romping in the stables
Dan Mahoney's "Black and White", Ian Rankin's Rebus
All these books have made the authors famous

If you've got a little time to spare, try and read a book
Why bother with the telly. It isn't worth a look
A book your imagination will expound
A really good book, you can't put down

A Fireman

A fireman is my hero, in wellies and hard hat
He slides down that pole, just like that
Once the siren goes, in that engine he doth race
Not knowing what awaits him, what sights he has to face
To do his job he must be brave

Using a fireman's lift he carries victims down
Balancing on a ladder, from the roof down to the ground
He battles with fires and thick black smoke
Sometimes gets hurt, sometimes chokes
A fireman is one of the elite
Very courageous, any fire, he'll defeat

Builders

Builders build things, this we all know
Brick upon brick in neat measured rows
Very soon houses appear, a welcomed sight
New homes for people whose future looks bright
Women ogle them as bare chested they work
To catch sight of their bum is an added perk
Broad of shoulders with strong muscled arms
They can also turn on the charm
They really are the salt of the earth
Their expertise we acknowledge, we value their worth

Electricians

Electricians need to be sure
Or a shock they will endure
Cables and switches attached to the mains
Dangerous electricity is their domain
They wire houses and buildings too
Theirs is a skill acquired by few
When things go wrong we are left in the dark
Or a fire gets started by a small spark
It is imperative that they do their work right
As electricity is a powerful might

Farmers

Farmers live on farms, they work the land
The life they lead isn't very grand
As they work really hard tending cattle and sheep
Throughout the year they plant and reap
They claim they are poor, believe me they are rich
Owning tractors, big cars and rivers with fish
They certainly are a breed apart
They can all sing and they dress real smart
They also have a permanent smile on their face
As they endeavour to sustain the human race

Crystal Ball

Oh if I could look into a crystal ball to see what tomorrow will bring
I could then avoid all the pitfalls and to a peaceful existence could cling
I would plan my day to suit myself without a thought for others
It would be bliss to live my life, pre-planned to avoid all bothers

Keys

Keys play an important part in my life
As criminal behaviour and thieves are rife
I lock the doors to protect my assets
Personal safety is also a facet

The car key I use every day
Prior to my driving away
I lock the door when the car I park
No joy riding in it, for a lark

In my diary all my secrets are kept
I keep it locked, my thoughts to protect
To lock my jewellery box is a must
Is there no one I can trust?

Keys are very important to me
Without them where would I be?
My house, my possessions I must secure
As a nervous breakdown I couldn't endure

British

Englishmen

Englishmen are handsome, I like the way they speak
They strut and pose, they are certainly not meek
Their confidence is high, they are proud of who they are
They are tall and able and look just like film stars
Sworn enemies in rugby, we shout and call them names
We don't like it when they're winning all the games
The problem is their attitude, they make us feel inferior
Whilst in reality they are not our superior
However, we are British and united we would stand
Should it prove necessary to defend this glorious land

Scotsmen

Scotsmen are tall, sturdy and strong
Even wearing kilts they can do no wrong
Very patriotic, home rule their decree
They are Celts just like you and me,
They live where the terrain is mountainous and rough
To survive the weather they have to be tough
Those bagpipes they play, blows my mind
The noise they make is hard to define
Playing rugby, we don't mind if they win
Although to lose is a mortal sin
We have bonded with the clans north of the border
The Welsh, the Scots, we are of one order

Irishmen

Short and wiry, eyes of blue

Black hair, red hair, curly too

They epitomise charm, no snakes on their land

An Irish navvy gave me my first kiss on the hand

The dancing Irish, they are world class

Boy bands, girl bands, they amass

Playing rugby, they have speed and flair

Very difficult to beat, they always play fair

I feel very sad for our Irish friends

The troubles, I cannot comprehend

How an Irishman can kill an Irishman, I'll never know

With foreign wars looming, the seeds of peace they should sow

With us Welsh, the Irish have struck a cord

As our ancestors also suffered at the hands of the lords

Welshmen

Short of stature, but strong of heart

The Welsh are a breed apart

As Dafydd Iwan sings 'We are still here'

And the likes of Ann Robinson we do not fear

We have fought to keep the Welsh language alive

We have succeeded as it continues to thrive

The Welsh who achieve become the world's best

Head and shoulders above the rest

When it comes to rugby, for glory they thirst

And when they lose, the Welsh nation hurts

Male voice choirs in abundance are found

Producing a unique, distinctive sound

We in Wales are Welsh first, British second

That is the way it will stay, I reckon

Three Generations - Progress

My grandmother had thirteen children when birth control was to astain
Money was scarce, struggling to survive was the aim
Three of her children died, two from diphtheria
I count my blessings when I think of her

She did her washing by hand, made her own bread
There was a lack of opportunities, her gifted children were fed
Family life was important with religion to the fore
Their sense of values correct, no need to lock front doors

My mother fared a little better, progress had been made
She had four children, took in washing to get paid
We had a bathroom in our house, an outside loo
It was rented accommodation, houses owned by few

It was a struggle but a free education we received
No servile work for us, my mother was so pleased
A washer and a Hoover she had in later years
And when she had a television, her eyes just filled with tears

Is my life so much better? Two children I have had
I own my car, my house, I've no reason to be sad
Central heating, freezers, videos have now become essentials
Computers and dishwashers have become so consequential

However, life is stressful, our streets no longer safe
Children are the targets for murder, abuse and rape
Family life has suffered as mothers go to work
To keep up with society, to obtain unnecessary perks

We have now become too clever, we explore outer space
Children cloned, mobile phones, life's pace is now a race
We need to re-evaluate our priorities in life
As populations starve, with Aids and Cancers rife

On reflection there are lessons to be learnt, from days gone by
Lost family values and religion we should endeavour to revive
Unless we do, life on earth will only get worse
And our brilliance and inventiveness will become a wasteful curse

Essex Wives

Those Essex Wives have lost the plot
All they think of, is what haven't I got?
What they have got is Gucci shoes on their feet
With matching bags and luggage neat
Gymnasium visits to stop bottoms sagging
A Mercedes Benz to carry the shopping
Walk-in wardrobes are also their thing
To hold Versace clothes, necklaces, rings
Hair pampered two or three times a week
Executive husbands working hard to them keep
Two or three children attending elite schools
To become upper class twits and over us rule
Have Essex wives lost the plot?
Suddenly, I feel, no they have not

Music

Music is inside my veins
On hearing it I move and sway
I've only got to hear the beat
To start tapping with my size 4 feet

'Imagine' by John Lennon is my number one
McCartney's 'Yesterday' had a good run
I like Enrique Iglesias' romantic song 'Hero'
Also, Julian Lloyd Webber's music on Cello
Music is inside my veins
On hearing it I move and sway

Male voice choirs are also my thing
My heart starts pounding when 'Jacob's ladder' they sing
Their rendering of Myfanwy when voices soar
Always ensures a deserving encore
Music is inside my veins
On hearing it I move and sway

I like Pavarotti, Carreras, Plácido Domingo
Robbie Williams, piano concertos
Russell Watson's 'Pearl Fisherman's' duet
Handel's largo, clarinets
Music is inside my veins
On hearing it I move and sway

Music soothes the savaged breast
Orchestral music is the best
Brass bands with their versatility
Fill a niche with creativity
Music is inside my veins
On hearing it I move and sway

Healthy Eating

No chocolate, no cakes
No pasties, no Flakes
Drinking eight glasses of water each day
Eating five portions of fruit of different array
No red meat, no lamb
Only chicken or ham
I'm doing everything I should
I'm looking great but life ain't good

Choice

If you have a choice to make
Take your time, slow down the pace
Weigh up all the pros and cons
Else you'll get the wrong response

I know that you've been hurt before
This time around you must be sure
Your heart will tell you what is right
So take your time and raise your sights

Is it really what you want?
Have you really struck a bond?
Life's too short to stand and dither
Tell her that you want and need her
As deep down you know it's true
It is her fate to be with you

Family Life

My mother brought us up on ten shillings a week
She had the rent to pay and four girls to keep
My father was forty six when he passed away
He suffered from lung disease until his dying day

His working down the coal mines caused the problems you see
And there was no social security to give handouts free
But we were brought up with religion in mind
To be clean and healthy, polite and kind

We had no toys, I wore hand me down clothes
As did all my friends, we were happy I suppose
However, it taught us to value what we had
A good loving mother and that wasn't bad

Now we are grown up and have made our own way
All married, fairly affluent, good jobs we have held sway
Our parents would be proud of us - the straight and narrow our domain
But in our memories, the bad times remain

Shopping

I have my plastics inside my purse
Are they a blessing or are they a curse?
I am ready to do my weekly shopping
And once I start there is no stopping
There is no limit on my credit you see
So my spending control is all up to me

I shop and think of all the points that I'll get
Five hundred and fifty is the most I've had yet
The money vouchers I subsequently receive
Are all geared up for my brain to deceive
As I believe I am richer than I am
Until I realise it is all a scam

These plastics, these points, but what the heck
Do I need to do a bank statement check?
For I have my plastics inside my purse
And have suddenly decided they are not a curse

God

If you are feeling lonely turn to God and say a prayer
Wherever you may be, you will find he is always there
His presence you will feel, his warmth will you surround
He will make you feel secure, his love will be profound

If your load is heavy turn to God and say a prayer
He will lighten up your spirits and your problem you will bear
To know one is not alone is a blessing given to the few
Who know that God is there, every day for me and you

If you are feeling weary turn to God and say a prayer
He will give you strength, he will show you that he cares
Life's path is never easy, God's message you must heed
God will never fail you, he is there in time of need

He is a friend you can rely on, so afraid you will never be
He gave his only son, to die for you and me
To give you life eternal, to give you heavenly bliss
There is no greater love than this

My Car

My pride and joy is my little red car
A Peugeot 106, she is a star
I sit and drive behind the wheel
Feeling like Boadicea, the Warrior Queen

Off we go, I put my foot on the throttle
We've got to show a bit of bottle
Overtaking on a nasty bend
Tailgating a Mercedes Benz

The cameras, oh I them ignore
What speed am I doing? I'm really not sure
And those roundabouts, they are the pits
I drive straight through, like a true blue Brit

Red, amber, green the lights me confuse
I refuse to stop, the car ahead I pursue
An accident I have truly not had
So my driving isn't really that bad

We arrive home, the car I park
With the headlights on, as it is very dark
I turn off the engine, and lock the door
A pleasant journey? I'm really not sure
The good thing is, we're home safe and sound
As tomorrow again, we'll be outward bound

The Choir

I sing in the ladies choir
In search of excellence we aspire
Sopranos and altos just the two
Singing songs with arrangements new

The sopranos sing the melody
The altos sing in harmony
Learning the words can be a bind
But certainly keeps you healthy of mind

If you have time to spend in leisure
Join a choir, it will give you pleasure
Think of all the people that you'll meet
As against other choirs you compete

It can be hard work, it can also be fun
The pride you feel when praises won
You get to travel from place to place
Join a choir, stand the pace

The criteria is that you must be able to sing
As to the music your voice will ring
The other thing is, you must look good
Just as a chorister should

To sing with other choirs is an experience sublime
Everyone in good voice, standing in line
An appreciative audience, the accolade
Leaving you with memories that will never fade

Lazy

I open one eye, look at the clock
I am lying in bed, it is twelve o'clock
Shall I stay in bed or shall I get up
I switch on the teasmaid, I'll have a cup

I think I will laze for another hour
Then I'll have a refreshing shower
It is afternoon, I sit and watch TV
I ring for a takeaway, delivered to me

It is early evening, I am having a rest
I want to look my very best
As my lover is planning to visit
His stay is always very illicit

I haven't cleaned the house, but he won't mind
He understands that I am, very refined
So what does it matter if the house is a mess
He knows I hate work and this I confess

My mother will call tomorrow and do all the work
She will hoover and dust, she thinks I'm a jerk
She will wash and iron, all for free
Who is the wisest, her or me?

Love

Love knows no boundaries, one cannot love to order
Colour, creed and orientation have now crossed all the borders
Young with old, black with white, it is all to do with heart
It is obvious to us all that nothing will them part

Male with male has now become the norm
To heterosexual ways they are unable to conform
Likewise with the female species, lesbians they are called
They fall in love with women, it is their natures call

Love gives life purpose, its blessing we accrue
And who you fall in love with isn't always up to you
Call it fate or what you will, it was meant to be
Two hearts beating as one, no problems they foresee

They are very brave, the ones who deviate
But things are getting better, we now accept their fate
True love conquers all, we've got rid of old taboos
Which to lovers worldwide is very good news

Broody

Feeling broody, do be choosy
Don't go for a man who's boozy
Go for brains, don't go for brawn
Even if to beefcake drawn
Your offspring's future must be bright
Look around and do what's right
Go for someone of good breeding
To impregnate you with his seedling
Feeling broody, do be choosy

Mother

The bond between mother and child no one can ever sever
It binds you, holds you and it lasts forever
Your mother is your rock, she keeps your life on form
Her love it will embrace you, her love will keep you warm

She is always there for you in times of need and stress
Her thoughtful words, they comfort you in times of great distress
She will give you money, in her eyes you do no wrong
When doubts assail, her support will make you strong

If you have your mother, cherish her and care
As the time will come when she will not be there
Tell her that you love her every single day
No guilt will then torment you when her life has ebbed away

You only have one mother, you will survive when she is gone
Her influence will stay with you as you carry on
She has guided you and taught you what is right and what is wrong
You are her special person, unique among the throng

Aspirations

To college I must go and obtain a good degree
I've got my two 'A' Levels and some GCE's
I aim to have a good job and earn a lot of dosh
To enable me to live and dress like Spice Girl Posh
This is the only way as I haven't got a singing voice
Therefore, I am a girl limited of choice
To college I must go, and obtain a good drgree

Insurance

One day I know I'll die
This I fear my last sigh
Will an angel come for me?
To set my spirit free
To heaven I would like to go
Not that place of doom below
I'll have to pray to God tonight
Tell him that I've seen the light
The Ten Commandments I must heed
My remaining years to them concede
I already feel secure
As my future I've ensured

A Flame

To have a flame you must have a fire
The final one, the funeral pyre
Fire in your heart, to incite the Olympic flame
To motivate your quest for glory and fame
The flicker of a candle to light the way
Or else in the darkness you would have to stay

The rays of the sun can start a fire
Flames burning woodlands, conditions are dire
Starting with a fire, the flames will spread
Destroying all in its path, and the sky will turn red
To have a flame you must have a fire
The start of a fire is a flicker of flame

Free

The best things in life are free
Oh what bliss when my child hugs me
The first smile, the first word being 'mam'
Pushing my baby in the pram
A loving look from my handsome man
Good news following a medical scan
My child's winning the first prize
Receiving a gift as a surprise
We have no assets, we are poor
But we are happy, our love strong and sure
The best things in life are free
I am so glad I am me

My Way

Shall we go to Cardiff? Not if I have my way
I'd rather go to Swansea any day
Shall we go to Brecon? We'll go there by car
Not if I have my way, it is too far
Leave it to me, I'll plan our day
As we always end up doing things - my way

Touch

Let your fingers do the touching
More effective than the talking
As with your lover you do lie
Express your feelings, don't be shy
Touch her skin, is it smooth?
Her tired feelings you will soothe

If the surface is very rough
The terrain will make the going tough
Ascending a mountain or climbing a hill
Your fingers will seek, it is a climber's skill
Your personal safety, your touch will ensure
As a very bad fall would be hard to endure

Some like the touch and feel of leather
Raindrops on your hand when you check the weather
Is the heater warm, you check with your fingers
As to overcome the cold the heat must linger

The sense of touch the blind use to read
As their fingers over the Braille doth speed
They, more than most, value the sense of touch
They get on with their lives, they don't ask for much
I greatly admire these people, they never complain
As their independency they aim to sustain

Smell

We have a nose, we use it to smell
Is the food fresh, there is only one way to tell
If it smells awful, throw it away
Because if you consume it, the price you will pay

A pleasant smell is flowers in bloom
The fragrance you'll notice when you enter a room
Roses especially smell just right
They also are a beautiful sight

Women pay a high price for their scent
They consider it money well spent
The aroma hopefully will draw a man to their side
As their ultimate aim is to be a bride

Taste

Some things taste sweet, some things taste bitter
Eating fruit and vegetables will make you fitter
However, if the taste is not to your liking
You spit it out to avoid the eating
The gift of taste is a lasting pleasure
You acquire it young and it lasts forever

Education

Circumstances make you poor
Education is the cure
Qualifications will get you out of the mire
Leaving forever conditions dire

My Will

I am writing my will
I've already taken three headache pills
The problem is I've so little to leave
To my children and this doth me grieve
But there again, I won't be there
So why the hell should I care

Virginity

I am a virgin, I am still intact
I've not had a man and that's a fact
So if you know of someone out there for me
Send him my way, he can have it for free

Rock Bottom

When you are rock bottom there is only one way you can go
That is upwards and this you need to know
So do not get depressed as you have nothing to lose
Surely that is good news

Regret

We have all done something that we regret
When we think about it, we get upset
Looking back, it is too late
We shouldn't have done it, in the first place

Talent

If you have a talent handle it with care
Make use of it, nurture it, as you know it's there
It would be a travesty to ignore and let it die
From lack of use, what money cannot buy

Progress

Hotpoint washing machine, Dyson cleaner
All designed to make life easier
Heating at the flick of a switch
Why then do I have this nervous twitch?

Warning

You mess around with my son, I'll have your guts for garters
He's intelligent, he's handsome and that is just for starters
He's much too good for you, deep down you know that's true
I've got great plans for him and they don't include you

A Fag

I tried a fag, it was a drag
I tried a shag, it was a drag but better than the fag

An Affair

Oh what pain it is to discover
That my wife has taken a lover
What has he got that I haven't got?
A job, good looks, posh car, that's what

Suffering

Suffering is bearing pain, every day
Knowing full well that it won't go away
Stoically, the afflicted accepts their fate
With exemplary courage every day they face

The Sales

I must dash, the sales are on
Half price in the shops, it really is tres bon
Some kitchen chairs and a frock or two
It's the only time I can afford something new

A Hole

A hole is a space with nothing there
It is dangerous, one could fall in there
Once filled, the hole no longer exists
Consequently, it no longer poses a risk

Rain

Rain rain go away
I really don't need you today
As I've got my best frock on
And a raincoat I won't don

Satisfaction

Satisfaction you get after work well done
Even when no accolades won
Because you know you did your best
Under circumstances that did you test

Disappointment

Disappointment is a sinking feeling when your expectations are not met
From excited anticipation feelings plummet to the depth
Depression is the backlash until you pull yourself together
With the expectation that things can only get better

Sad

For years and years I have done a lot of good
Helped the less fortunate, as one should
But what I find really sad
Is that people only remember that one time I was bad

I Said

You must lose weight, I said
You must stop smoking, I said
You must get a job, I said
Get lost, he said

Fish

I would like to be a little fish swimming in the sea
Darting her, darting there, nowt to bother me
Swimming in a shoal, who would notice me
A little fish swimming in the sea

Nudist

A nudist I could never be
Starkers, well it just ain't me
My body, it looks better clothed
Imperfections not exposed

Deceit

It is heartbreaking to be deceived
Believing the sentiments received
The emotional trauma your heart doth break
As your money or love the traitor did take

Winning

The winner takes it all
The loser by the wayside fall
Glory you acquire when you become the best
Having beaten all the rest

Trust

Trust is a valuable commodity
Experienced by humans in its entirety
Trust once broken is gone forever
To let someone down is not very clever

Scandal

It was a scandal but that's nothing new
As it went on its way the story grew
The truth became lost, fact became fiction
And the two culprits smiled with great satisfaction

Testicles

Women haven't got them, you know that this is true
But you men do and they total two
They are the jewels in your crown, so I've been told
Apparently too, they are worth their weight in gold
So handle them with care, else your condition will become dire
And you'll end up singing in a ladies choir

Exams

I look at the paper, there s nothing written there
I am sitting an exam, at the questions I stare
My mind is blank I begin to sweat
The answers just haven't come to me yet
Who said that schooldays are the best
I bet that they haven't taken this bloody test

Suicide

She walked into the sea, all alone
Her brain befuddled, her heart turned to stone
She was tired of living, she wanted to die
T'was in the water she breathed her last sigh
But all was not lost she is now in God's care
At peace, no further torment or pain to bear

Endangered Species

I am an endangered species
I cook and iron clothes with creases
I don't smoke, I don't swear, I am faithful and true
Times have changed, I've become one of the few

Location

Do pick the right location
One with a solid foundation
Then your house can be erected
On the site that you've selected

Mistress

Look ahead, don't look at me
Your loving gaze they must not see
Alas, I am your bit on the side
Destined never to be a bride

Brainwave

I've just had a brainwave
Some money I must save
It's the only way that I'll get rich
Isn't life a bitch

Obedience

When we are young we are taught to obey
Obediently we listen and do as you say
Suddenly we begin to question the need
Disagreeing, we refuse to concede
It is what we call growing up
Deciding one day that enough is enough

Spectacles

I have had new specs, now I can see
Everything is so clear to me
I now see the dust on the telly, the mess on the floor
Even the scratches made by the dog, on the front door
I can see the lines on my face, the grey in my hair
Where are my old specs, they are better I swear

Swimming

I like the water, I learnt to swim in the sea
Swimming pools were non-existent in our vicinity
Swimming is really like riding a bike
Once you can do it, you can do it for life

Liar

You are a liar, it is sad but what can I say
We have learnt from past experiences the truth is not your way
However, you'll be sorry when one day the truth you'll speak
And no one will believe you, remembering past deceits

Homeless

All they want is a roof over their heads
Going to sleep in warm cosy beds
It isn't too much to ask for in this day and age
People sleeping rough is bad for our image

Chance

He who hesitates is lost
Left bereft to count the cost
Be prepared to take a chance
Your future prospects to enhance

Intruder

There is an intruder in my house
I hear it move and scuttle about
This intruder really bothers me
As its appearance I have yet to see
This intruder in my house
I am convinced is a little mouse

Enhancement

Collagen injections to her lips
Liposuction to her hips
Silicone implants to boost her breasts
Her nose reshaped, I do protest
As my wife I no longer know
As to the inevitable she refuses to bow

Attitude

Every day is a bonus
When old age is upon us
Enjoy every single day
As the grim reaper doth hold sway
You are never too old to dance
Go on holiday, take a chance
Attitude is all
The young of mind have a ball
Every day is a bonus
When old age is upon us

Sacrifice

On the cross his body bled
A crown of thorns upon his head
He died to save you and me
He took our sins, he set us free
Proof of God's love, this should suffice
As it was the ultimate sacrifice

Talent

I wish that I could paint
An artist I just ain't
I can't even draw a square
My efforts end with canvas bare
Lack of talent, there is no cure
I just ain't got it, that's for sure

A Scarecrow

Stone the crows, I've just seen a scarecrow
Propped up in a field, behind a hedgerow
The birds it is supposed to scare
Yet they perch on its head, without a care
What is the point of a man of straw
When it becomes a resting place for craws

Aggressiveness

Aggressiveness is puerile
It is so futile
It defeats the objective
Charm is more effective

Searching

I am searching, searching for that I cannot find
Is it love? Is it riches? No peace for restless mind
When I find that, for which I seek, I will know its worth
As I will be happy and contented, no further need to search

Wishful Thinking

Some people seem to have it all
Whilst others appear to take all the falls
However, do not hanker after the unattainable
Concentrate instead on the matters sustainable

Religion

What is religion to you or I?
Is it someone up there in the sky?
Or is it something deep within
Telling us what is or what isn't sin?

Standing Firm

Oh what feeling of elation
When you've resisted all temptation
With your conscience you did grapple
And your backbone stood the tackle

Patience

Patience you need when you wait in a queue
Of when your wife is shopping for something new
Tolerant! You have the patience of a saint
But there is s limit as a saint you just ain't

A Dream

A dream you must pursue to the end
As on your talents you can depend
Giving up would lead to a lifetimes regret
So take a chance and edge your bets

Reading

If you read, you can spell
Also a story you can tell
You don't read!! What a loss
A rolling stone gathers no moss

The Derby

I must pick a horse, it is Derby day
I place my bet, five pounds each way
If I lose, I won't feel remorse
Simply because I backed the wrong horse
As Derby day only comes round once a year
And I love to see the ladies in their fabulous gear

Breathing Space

Patience is a virtue
Give her time to get to know you
She needs a little breathing space
Ultimately, her love for you she'll face

Streakers

I must confess a streaker I have seen
At a rugby match, he was six foot four and lean
I didn't bat an eyelid, I have seen it all before
They are always on the telly, they are becoming quite a bore

Decisions

It is one thing or the other
Now is not the time to dither
Decision time, just do what's right
Allowing you to sleep at night

A Mouse

I am a little mouse with a long tail
As I scuttle about, behind me it trails
My soft cuddly body is tiny and so are my feet
I like to eat cheese with my very sharp teeth
The pity is I grow up to be a rat
And there is nothing I can do about that

Terrorists

Terrorists are a breed apart
They kill and maim, they have no heart
Brainwashed or not, it would be a sin
For us to give in to fear and let them win

My Brain

I've got a brain, so I'm often told
'Use your brain' my mother would scold
But how can I make it work for me
When this brain cannot see

Nature

Catastrophic devastation, everywhere
Following a ghastly nightmare
Hurricanes, Tornados, nature's force
Relentless, unstoppable, wildly off course
Beyond our control, we can only pray
That such an experience won't come our way

The Cuckoo

I am the cuckoo in this nest
Having got rid of all the rest
My adopted mother keeps me alive
This is how our species survives

Broody

Feeling broody, do be choosy
Don't go for a man who's boozy
Go for brains, don't go for brawn
Even if to beefcake drawn
Your offsprings future must be bright
Look around and do what's right
Feeling broody, do be choosy

Goodness Gracious Me

My daughter is pregnant, goodness gracious me
In nine months time what will that make me?
I am too young, I am only forth three
Me a grandmother, goodness gracious me!

The Wall

I am standing in front of a wall
The problem is I am not very tall
I cannot see what's on the other side
There is no gate and the wall is too wide
This barrier, this wall really bothers me
As it has raised my curiosity

Stealing

To steal is to take what is not thine
You have broken the law, you have crossed the line
A thief is what you have become
As to temptation you did succumb

Hope

Hope lingers eternal in the human breast
Even when a hopeless plight doth us severely test
When one loses hope there is nothing left
Nothing to cling on to, one is left bereft
So to be optimistic and things will turn out for the best
Use the hope that lingers in the human breast

The Ozone Layer

We must say a little prayer
For that hole in the ozone layer
Did I hear someone snigger
Take my word for it, it is getting bigger

Attraction

Goodness gracious me
Do you see what I see?
A handsome man staring at me
I am single, the question is, is he?

The Prize

It's the thrill of the chase
It's like winning a race
But the prize is for life
When she becomes your wife

Lovers

Who would believe it of those two
They were seen together so it must be true
Her with her lah de dah ways
Who would believe that she would stray
Him so handsome and debonair
Her so plain and dull I declare
They say that opposites attract
It is an indisputable fact
Good heavens who would believe it of those two

I Said

You must lose weight, I said
You must stop smoking, I said
You must get a job, I said
Get lost, he said

One Look

Just one look, that's all it took
My heart jumped, my legs just shook
You were a stranger, we had never even met
Love at first sight, this is the nearest to it yet

Disappointment

Disappointment is a sinking feeling when your expectations are not met
From excited anticipation feelings plummet to the depth
Depression is the backlash until you pull yourself together
With the expectation that things will only get better

Injustice

The award was given on merit
I did all the work, she took all the credit
I just let it happen, there was nothing I could do
As no one believed me, the question is, do you?

Julie

She is beautiful, blue eyed with shiny red hair
Very intelligent, at her people stare
She is generous, interesting, never unruly
She is my granddaughter, her name is Julie

Granddaughters

To see such beauty is very rare
People passing by, stop and stare
I am a little biased it is true
As Emma and Bethan are my granddaughters and they total two

A Lion

I am a lion, I have a big yellow mane
King of the jungle, over other beasts I reign
I roar and growl when I am angry
I hunt and kills when I am hungry
A pride of lions is a magnificent sight
All who see them would be wise to take flight

Folk

There is nowt as strange as folk they say
And a few have come my way
The selfish, the prejudiced, the rude, the unkind
The feeble, the strong, the weak of mind
But in times of crisis they rally around
It is then that you find the good that abounds

Little

Little houses in little villages
With little shops, and little schools
For little children with little voices
And little people with little choices

Humour

I have got a sense of humour, it has been my saving grace
Keeping me on track when stressful times I've had to face
Even in my darkest hour I found that I could smile
To cover all the heartache, it was just my style
When God dished out this humour, he gave me more than most
A valuable, priceless asset of which I'm proud to boast
I have got a sense of humour, it always stands me in good stead
I smile in the face of adversity and all my fears are shed

Home

A house is not a home unless your mother's there
It is only bricks and mortar and this I do declare
When mother passed away she left the homestead standing
Heartless, it has now become just another building